STOP NEGAT.

HALT THAT THOUGHT

Choose To Leave Out Thoughts
That Only Harm and Hurt

Kay Cox

Table of Contents

Chapter 1:

You're Good Enough

People come and say 'I did something stupid today. I am so bad at this. Why is it always me?' You will acknowledge even if no one else says it, we often say it to ourselves.

So what if we did something stupid or somewhat a little awkward. I am sure no one tries to do such things voluntarily. Things happen and sometimes we cause them because we have a tendency to go out of our way sometimes. Or sometimes our ways have a possibility of making things strange.

It doesn't make you look stupid or dumb or ugly or less competent. These are the things you make up of yourself. I am not saying people don't judge. They do. But their judgment should not make you think less of yourself.

No matter how much you slip up, you must not stop and you must not bow down to some critique. You only have to be a little determined and content with yourself that you have got it alright.

You need to realize your true potential because no matter what anyone says, you have what it takes to get to the top.

Need some proof? Ask yourself, have you had a full belly today? Have you had a good night's sleep last night? Have you had the will and energy to get up and appear for your job and duties? Have you had the guts to ask someone out to dinner because you had a crush on them?

If you have a good answer to any of these questions, and you have done it all on your own with your efforts. Congratulations my friend, you are ready to appraise yourself.

You have now come to terms with your abilities and you don't need anyone else's approval or appraisal. You don't depend on anyone either psychologically or emotionally.

So now when the times get tough you can remind yourself that you went through it before. And even if you failed back then, you have the right energy and right state of mind to get on top of it now. You are now well equipped to get ahead of things and be a better person than you were the last time.

You are enough for everything good or not so good happening in and around you.

Your health, your relations, your carrier, your future. Everything can be good and better when you have straightened out your relationship with yourself. When you have found ways to talk to yourself ad make yourself realize your true importance. When you learn to admire yourself.

Once you learn to be your best critic, you can achieve anything. Without ever second-guessing yourself and ever trying to care for what anyone else will think.

If you find yourself in a position where you had your heart broken but you still kept it open, you should have a smile on your face. Because now you might be on your path to becoming a superior human being.

Chapter 2:

Get Rid of Worry and Focus On The Work

Worry is the active process of bringing one's fears into reality.

Worrying about problems halts productivity by taking your mind off the work in hand.

If you're not careful, a chronic state of worrying can lead you down a dark path that you might find hard to get out of.

Always focus on the required work and required action towards your dream.

Anything could happen, good or bad,

but if you remain focused and do the work despite the problems,

you will through with persistence and succeed.

Always keep your mind on the goal,

your eyes on the prize.

Have an unwavering faith in your abilities no matter what.

Plan for the obvious obstacles that could stand in your way,

but never worry about them until you have to face them.

Tackle it with confidence as they come and move forward with pride.

Problems are bound to arise.

Respond to them necessarily along the way, if they actually happen.

After all, most worries never make it into reality.

Instead focus on what could go right.

Focus on how you can create an environment that will improve your chances of success.

You have the power over your own life and direction.

As children we dreamed big.

We didn't think about all the things that could go wrong.

As children we only saw the possibilities.

We were persistent in getting what we wanted no matter the cost.

As adults we need to be reminded of that child-like faith.

To crush worry as if it were never there.

To only focus on the possibilities.

You cannot be positive and negative at the same time.

You cannot be worrying and hopeful of the future.

You cannot visualise your perfect life while worrying about everything that could go wrong.

Choose one.

Stick to it.

Choose to concentrate on the work.

The result will take care of your worries.

Catch yourself when you feel yourself beginning to worry about things.

Instead of dwelling on the problem, choose to double down on the action.

Stay focused and steadfast in the vision of your ultimate goal.

The work now that you must do is the stepping stones to your success.

The work now must have your immediate attention.

The work now requires you to cast worry aside in favour of concentration and focus.

How many stepping stones are you away?

What is next?

Push yourself every single day.

Because only you have the power to create your future.

If not, things will remain the same as they have always been.

Always have a clearly defined goal,

A strong measure of faith,

And an equally strong measure of persistence and grit.

These are the ingredients to creating the life you want.

A life of lasting happiness and success.

Take control instead of accepting things as they are.

Reject anything else that is not the goal that you've set for yourself.

Whatever goal you set, ten times it, and focus on it every day.

The focus will keep your mind on the work until you succeed.

There will be no time to worry when you are too busy taking constant action.

Always have the belief In your heart and soul that you will succeed.

Never let a grain of doubt cast a shadow in your eventual path to victory.

Focus is key to all.

What you focus on, you will create.

Worrying is worse than useless,

it is DETRIMENTAL to your future.

Take control of your thoughts.

When worry pops it's ugly head, force it out with a positive thought of your future.

Don't let the negative illusions of worry live rent-free in your mind.

You are in control here.

Of what you watch,

What you read,

What you listen too

And what you think.

What you think of consistently will become.

Focus on what you want, and how to get there is crucial for lasting happiness and success.

Chapter 3:

Stop Dwelling on Things

It's 5 p.m., the deadline for an important work project is at 6, and all you can think about is the fight you had with the next-door neighbor this morning. You're dwelling. "It's natural to look inward," but while most people pull out when they've done it enough, an overthinker will stay in the loop."

Ruminating regularly often leads to depression. So, if you're prone to obsessing (and you know who you are), try these tactics to head off the next full-tilt mental spin cycle...

1.Distract Yourself

Go and exercise, scrub the bathtub spotless, put on music and dance, do whatever engrosses you, and do it for at least 10 minutes. That's the minimum time required to break a cycle of thoughts.

2.Make a Date to Dwell

Tell yourself you can obsess all you want from 6 to 7 p.m., but until then, you're banned. "By 6 p.m., you'll probably be able to think things through more clearly,"

3. 3 Minutes of Mindfulness

For one minute, eyes closed, acknowledge all the thoughts going through your mind. For the next minute, just focus on your breathing. Spend the last minute expanding your awareness from your breath to your entire body. "Paying attention in this way gives you the room to see the questions you're asking yourself with less urgency and to reconsider them from a different perspective,"

4.The Best and Worst Scenarios

Ask yourself...

"What's the worst that could happen?" and "How would I cope?" Visualizing yourself handling the most extreme outcome should alleviate some anxiety. Then consider the likelihood that the worst will occur.

Next, imagine the best possible outcome; by this point, you'll be in a more positive frame of mind and better able to assess the situation more realistically.

5. Call a Friend

Ask a friend or relative to be your point person when your thoughts start to speed out of control.

6. Is it worth it?

If you find that your mind is fixated on a certain situation, ask yourself if the dwelling is worth your time.

'Ask yourself if looking over a certain situation will help you accept it, learn from it and find closure,' 'If the answer is no, you should make a conscious effort to shelve the issue and move on from it.'

7. Identify your anxiety trigger

There may be a pattern in your worries, and this means you can help identify potential causes and use practice preventative measures.

'For many of us, rumination will occur after a trigger, so it is important to identify what it is,' 'For example, if you have to give a presentation at work and the last one you didn't go to plan, this can cause rumination and anxiety.

Chapter 4:

Seven Habits of Mentally Strong People

Mentally strong people also have great character and charming personalities because they can handle what ordinary people may not handle. Mental strength is the most desired trait by most people. To some, it is innate but others cultivate it over time through education or the school of life. Whichever way it is acquired, there are underlying habits that mentally strong people share.

Here are seven habits of mentally strong people:

1. ### They Are Forgiving

To err is human but forgiveness is divine. Forgiveness is difficult for most people to commit. It is seen as a sign of weakness but this is a fallacy. The contrary is true. Forgiveness is a measure of strength. When one person grossly transgresses another, the offended party will seek vengeance. He/she feels justified to revenge and until the offender 'pays' for his mistakes, the spirit of the offended will know no rest.

Mentally strong people are capable of forgiveness. This distinguishes them from the rest of the population. They understand that there is no point in re-visiting a matter when they can shelf it and prevent its repeat in the future. It does not mean that the offender has the license to continue hurting the other person. Instead, forgiveness sets the precedence that you are unaffected by the acts of an inconsiderate person. It demonstrates that your reasoning and emotions are not manipulated at will by someone who hurts you.

The next time someone wrongs you, let vengeance take the back seat and reason prevail over your actions. It is what mentally strong people do.

2. They Are Readers

There is nothing new under the sun. Everything that happens is a repetition of something that once occurred. To acquaint yourself with how history judged those who were once in your shoes, flip the pages of books and learn the signs of the time.

The habit of reading is not only for the literate. Even the illiterate can read, not books but the signs of the time and the harsh judgment of history on failures of men. Mentally strong people are wise not to learn from their mistakes but those of others. They unlearn the habits of failures and learn those of the successful.

Readership is a dynamic habit that is perfected by the mentally strong. They read the prevailing situations and adjust their actions accordingly. Reading builds the wealth of experience in life and prepares one on what action to take when confronted by a situation.

3. They Accept Criticism and Correction

Acceptance of correction from an authority displays humility. Correction and positive criticism are not to display your ignorance to the public but instead to inform you on a matter you were once ignorant about. Many people take criticism negatively and want to justify their actions. It is not always about being right or wrong – a concept that most people miss.

Embracing correction distinguishes mentally strong people from the faint-hearted who always rush to justify their acts.

The intelligence of the mentally strong is belittled when they engage in supremacy battles. They rise above the hate and become big brothers/sisters. Only a handful of a population can own up to their misinformation on a matter and humbly accept correction. Mentally strong people can display such levels of maturity.

4.   They Are Not Easily Discouraged

It takes a lot to discourage mentally strong people. While ordinary people are stoppable in their tracks, it is not the same for the mentally strong. They are resilient to the adversity of whatever nature. They pursue their targets viciously and settle at nothing short of victory.

Mentally strong people may face a thousand ways to die but survive every one of them. They have the proverbial nine lives of the cat. Their determination is unmatched making them the envy of their peers who give up easily when challenged.

The majority of people in their curriculum vitae say that they can work under pressure. Unfortunately, their breaking point reaches sooner than expected. In the face of immense pressure at work, they yield to frivolous and unrealistic demands meted on them by busybodies. This is not the portion of the mentally strong.

5.   They Are Innovative

Mentally strong people are not satisfied with the status quo. They always seek to unsettle the ordinary way of doing things. The traditional handling of affairs does not ogre well with them. There is always a new way of doing things.

Their mental strength is partly responsible for the adventurous spirit. The mentally endowed put their brains to work in solving human problems. They innovate simple life hacks, technology and come up with homemade solutions that were unknown before.

Innovation is not limited to the complicated science of experts. It also involves finding the simplest ways of solving problems in society. Innovation is habitual for mentally strong people.

6. They See The Bigger Picture

Life is a hunt for resources. Similar to the Lion, Mentally strong people do not lose focus of the antelope because of a dashing squirrel. To them, the point of reference is always the bigger picture. They interrogate every matter diligently to read between the lines because the devil always lies in the details.

It is not a matter of the emotions invoked in a discussion but the quality of reasoning devoid of any feelings. Mentally strong people can sieve needs from wants and decant fallacies from discussions.

7. They Are Bold

Fortune favors the bold. It is one thing to be decisive and another to boldly speak out your thoughts. Timidity is for mental infants (no offense). Mentally strong people are not afraid of giving their inputs in forums whenever required to because they speak from a point of knowledge.

Fearlessly talking about social ills and injustices is uncommon even among the political class. They lack the mental strength to engage fruitfully in matters of national importance. The bold is unafraid of how they may be challenged by other people because they are capable of seeing everybody's point of view. They appreciate the diversity in opinions.

The above are seven habits of mentally strong people. Mental strength wields untold power to those who possess it.

Chapter 5:

How To Worry Less

How many of you worry about little things that affect the way you go about your day? That when you're out with your friends having a good time or just carrying out your daily activities, when out of nowhere a sudden burst of sadness enters your heart and mind and immediately you start to think about the worries and troubles you are facing. It is like you're fighting to stay positive and just enjoy your day but your mind just won't let you. It becomes a tug of war or a battle to see who wins?

How many of you also lose sleep because your mind starts racing at bedtime and you're flooded with sad feelings of uncertainty, despair, worthlessness or other negative emotions that when you wake up, that feeling of dread immediately overwhelms you and you just feel like life is too difficult and you just dont want to get out of bed.

Well If you have felt those things or are feeling those things right now, I want to tell you you're not alone. Because I too struggle with those feelings or emotions on a regular basis.

At the time of writing this, I was faced with many uncertainties in life. My business had just ran into some problems, my stocks weren't doing well, I had lost money, my bank account was telling me I wasn't good enough, but most importantly, i had lost confidence. I had lost the ability to face each day with confidence that things will get better. I felt that i was worthless and that bad things will always happen to me. I kept seeing the negative side of things and it took a great deal of emotional toll on me. It wasn't like i chose to think and feel these things, but they just came into my mind whenever they liked. It was like a parasite feeding off my negative energy and thriving on it, and weakening me at the same time.

Now your struggles may be different. You may have a totally different set of circumstances and struggles that you're facing, but the underlying issue is the same. We all go through times of despair, worry, frustration, and uncertainty. And it's totally normal and we shouldn't feel ashamed of it but to accept that it is a part of life and part of our reality.

But there are things we can do to minimise these worries and to shift to a healthier thought pattern that increases our ability to fight off these negative emotions.

I want to give you 5 actionable steps that you can take to worry less and be happier. And these steps are interlinked that can be carried out in fluid succession for the greatest benefit to you. But of course you can choose whichever ones speaks the most to you and it is more important that you are able to practice any one of these steps consistently rather than doing all 5 of them haphazardly. But I want to make sure I give you all the tools so that you can make the best decisions for yourself.

Try this with me right now as I go through these 5 steps and experience the benefit for yourself instead of waiting until something bad happens.

The very first step is simple. Just breathe. When a terrible feeling of sadness rushes into your body out of nowhere, take that as a cue to close your eyes, stop whatever you are doing, and take 5 deep breathes through your nose. Breathing into your chest and diaphragm. Deep breathing has the physiological benefit of calming your nerves and releasing tension in the body and it is a quick way to block out your negative thoughts. Pause the video if you need to do practice your deep breathing before we move on.

And as you deep breathe, begin the second step. Which is to practice gratefulness. Be grateful for what you already have instead of what you think u need to have to be happy. You could be grateful for your dog, your family, your friends, and whatever means the most to you. And if you cannot think of anything to be grateful for, just be grateful that you are even alive and walking on this earth today because that is special and amazing in its own right.

Next is to practice love and kindness to yourself. You are too special and too important to be so cruel to yourself. You deserve to be loved and you owe it to yourself to be kind and forgiving. Life is tough as it is, don't make it harder. If you don't believe in yourself, I believe in you and I believe in your worthiness as a person that you have a lot left to give.

The fourth step is to Live Everyday as if it were your last. Ask yourself, will you still want to spend your time worrying about things out of your control if it was your last day on earth? Will you be able to forgive yourself if you spent 23 out of the last 24 hours of your life worrying? Or will you choose to make the most out of the day by doing things that are meaningful and to practice love to your family, friends, and yourself?

Finally, I just want you to believe in yourself and Have hope that whatever actions you are taking now will bear fruition in the future. That they will not be in vain. That at the end of the day, you have done everything to the very best of your ability and you will have no regrets and you have left no stone unturned.

How do you feel now? Do you feel that it has helped at least a little or even a lot in shaping how you view things now? That you can shift your perspective and focus on the positives instead of the worries?

If it has worked for you today, I want to challenge you to consistently practice as many of these 5 steps throughout your daily lives every single day. When you feel a deep sadness coming over you, come back to this video if you need guidance, or practice these steps if you remember them on your own.

Chapter 6:

If Today Was Your Last Day

If today was your last day, what would you do with your life? Steve Jobs once said that "For the past 33 years, I have looked in trhe mirror every morning and asked myself: '**If today** were the **last day** of my life, would I want to do what I am about to do **today**? ' And whenever the answer has been 'No' for too many **days** in a row, I know I need to change something.".

Do you agree with that statement? For me I believe that it is true to a certain extent. I argue that not many of us have the luxury of doing what we love to do every single day. As much as we want to work at that dream job or earn that great salary, or whatever that ideal may be, for some of us who have to feed a family or make ends meet, it is just not possible. And we choose to make that sacrifice to work at a job that we may not like, or go through a routine that sometimes might seem a drag. But that's a personal choice that we choose to make and that is okay too.

On the flip side, i do believe that for those who have the luxury and the choice to pursue whatever careers, dreams, hobbies, and interests we want to pursue, that we should go for it and not live life in regret. I have heard of countless friends who work at a job they hate day in and day out, complaining about their life every single day and about how miserable they are, but are too afraid to leave that job in fear of not being able to find something they like or in fear that their dreams would not work out. Not because they couldn't afford to do so, but because they are afraid. This fear keeps them trapped in a never ending cycle of unhappiness and missed opportunities.

Personally, I'm in the camp of doing something you dislike even if u struggle with it if it can provide you with some financial security and pay your bills, whilst at the same time pursuing your dreams part time just to test the waters. You have the comfort of a monthly stream of income while also taking a leap of faith and going after what you really want to do in life. And who knows it could work out some day. In the present moment, I'm actually working on many different interests and hobbies. I do the necessary work that i hate but explore other areas that brings me joy, and that is what keeps be going. I have a passion for singing, songwriting, tennis, and making videos like this that not only educates but also aims to bring joy to others. My full-time job only fulfils my bank account while my interests and work that i do on the side fulfils my heart and soul. And who knows, if any one of these side hobbies turn out into something that I can make some money with, hey it's a win win situation now don't you think?

I challenge each and every one of you to go ahead and take a leap of faith. Time waits for no one and you never know when your last day might be. Koby Bryant died suddenly from a helicopter crash at a young age of 41. But I would argue that because he pursued his dreams at a young age, he has already lived a wonderful and fulfilling life as opposed to someone who is too afraid to do what they want and hasn't lived up to their fullest potential despite living until 90. You have also heard of Chadwick Boseman who was immortalised as a great human being who gave it his all despite fighting colon cancer. He pursued his dreams and I bet that he had no regrets that his life had to end earlier than it should. And to Steve jobs, he gave us Apple, the biggest company in the world by pursuing his dream of changing the world and the way we communicate with one another. Without him we wouldn't have all our favourite beloved apple products that we use today. Without him there might not be amazon, google, Facebook because there wouldn't be apps and there wouldn't be devices that people used to do all these things with.

But most importantly, this is about you. How do you want to live your life, and if today was your last day, what would you do differently and how would this carry on to all other areas of your life. Your relationships with your family, your relationship with your friends, your partner. And do you feel fulfilled as a human being or do you feel empty inside. It is never too late to turn your life around and make choices that will make your heart fill with immense joy and gratitude until your life truly ends. So make the decision right now to honour yourself by living your day to the fullest, coz you never know when it might be your last.

Chapter 7:

5 STEPS TO HELP YOU CHOOSE YOUR WORD OF THE YEAR

Here are a few easy steps to help guide you in choosing your 2021 word of the year.

Step 1: Reflect

The first thing I want you to do is to reflect on this past year and ask yourself these questions. Jot down whatever pops into your head without self-editing.

What could I use more of in my life?

What could I use less of in my life?

What characteristics would I like to have?

By the end of the day, I feel (fill in the blank).

How do i want to feel?

Once you review your responses, you'll have a better sense of the direction you'd like to go, or what you feel may be lacking in your life.

Step 2: Visualize

Visualize what the perfect day would feel like; the emphasis here is **"feel**." think about how you want your morning routine to feel, how you want to feel at work or throughout the day, and how you want to feel right before you go to bed.

I also recommend meditating or sitting in silence for a couple of minutes and asking yourself, "what word do i want to focus on in 2021?". This is simple but effective.

I think this exercise works best when you're in a relaxed state. If you're having trouble maybe try it before you go to sleep or first thing in the morning. You could also turn on an aromatherapy diffuser, light a candle, or put some calming music on in the background. You'd be amazed how being still can help your intuition shine through, and bring your word to the forefront.

Step 3: Create A List

Spend 10 minutes creating a list of the words that come to mind, no self-editing!

Step 4: Review & Refine

Review your list and narrow down your favorites. **I'd circle or highlight 3 words.**

Chances are you'll see a theme going on between the words you wrote down. Do any of the words jump out at you, make you feel excited, nervous, scared, uncomfortable, or at ease? Sometimes the words that scare us most can mean we're on the right track because change isn't always easy. At the same time, i think finding your word can also bring peace and empowerment.

Think about the words, try them on, and see what feels right. No need to over-analyze this process, trust your gut instead. Gently review your list and let the words pick you.

Step 5: Ask Yourself This Very Important Question

Now that you narrowed down your list to three words, there's just one more question to ask:

Are you interested, or are you committed?

I heard this question in a video i watched. So tell me, are you interested in your word, or are you committed? If you're merely "interested," then chances are you'll make excuses as to why you're not putting forth the effort to *actually* make changes. But if you're "committed" to your word, you'll do whatever it takes to implement that word and bring more of it into your life. If necessary, allow yourself a day or two, even a week, to think about this.

Chapter 8:

How To Succeed In Life

"You can't climb the ladder of success with your hands in your pocket."

Every day that you're living, make a habit of making the most out of it. Make a habit of winning today. Don't dwell on the past, don't worry about the future. You just have to make sure that you're winning today. Move a little forward every day; take a little step every day. And when you're giving your fruitful efforts, you're making sure you're achieving your day, then you start to built confidence within yourselves. Confidence is when you close your eyes at night and see a vision, a dream, a goal, and you believe that you're going to achieve it. When you're doing things, when you're productive the whole day, then that long journey will become short in a matter of time.

Make yourself a power list for each day. Take a sheet of paper, write Monday on top of it and then write five critical, productive, actionable tasks that you're going to do that day. After doing the task, cross it off. Repeat the process every day of every week of every month till you get closer to achieving your goals, your dreams. It doesn't matter if you're doing the same tasks every day or how minor or major they are; what matters is that it's creating momentum in things that you've believed you couldn't do. And as soon as the momentum gets completed, you start to believe that you can do something. You eventually stop writing your tasks down because now they've become your new habits. You need a reminder for them. You don't need to cross them off because you're going to do them. The power list helps you win the day. You're stepping out of your comfort zone, doing something that looks uncomfortable for starters, but while doing this, even for a year, you will see yourself standing five years from where you're standing today.

Decide, commit, act, succeed, repeat. If you want to be an inspiration to others, a motivator to others, impact others somehow, you have to self-evaluate certain perceptions and think that'll help you change the way you see yourself and the world. Perseverance, hard-working, and consistency would be the keywords if one were to achieve success in life. You just have to keep yourself focused on your ultimate goal. You will fall a hundred times. There's always stumbling on the way. But if you have the skill, the power, the instinct to get yourself back up every time you fall, and to dig yourself out of the whole, then no one can stop you. You have to control the situation, Don't ever let the situation control you. You're living life exactly as it should be. If you don't like what you're living in, then consider changing the aspects. The person you are right now versus the person you want to be in the future, there's only a fine line between the two that you have to come face-to-face with.

Your creativity is at most powerful the moment you open your eyes and start your day. That's when you get the opportunity to steer your emotions and thoughts in the direction that you want them to go, not the other way around. Every failure is a step closer to success. We won't succeed on the first try, and we will never have it perfect by trying it only once. But we can master the art of not giving up. We dare to take risks. If we never fail, we never get the chance of getting something we never had. We can never taste the fruits of success without falling. The difference between successful people and those who aren't successful is the point of giving up.

Success isn't about perfection. Instead, it's about getting out of bed each day, clearing the dust off you, and thinking like a champion, a winner, going on about your day, being productive, and making the most out of it. Remember that the mind controls your body; your body doesn't hold your mind. You have to make yourself mentally tough to overcome the fears and challenges that come in the way of your goals. As soon as you get up in the morning, start thinking about anything or anyone that you're grateful for. Your focus should be on making yourself feel good and confident enough to get yourself through the day.

The negative emotions that we experience, like pain or rejection, or frustration, cannot always make our lives miserable. Instead, we can consider them as our most incredible friends that'll drive us to success. When people succeed, they tend to party. When they fail, they tend to ponder. And the pondering helps us get the most victories in our lives. You're here, into another day, still breathing fine, that means you got another chance, to better yourself, to be able to right your wrongs. Everyone has a more significant potential than the roles they put themselves in.

Trust yourself always. Trust your instinct—no matter what or how anyone thinks. You're perfectly capable of doing things your way. Even if they go wrong, you always learn something from them. Don't ever listen to the naysayers. You've probably heard a million times that you can't do this and you can't do that, or it's never even been done before. So what? So what if no one has ever done it before. That's more of the reason for you to do it since you'll become the first person to do it. Change that 'You can't' into 'Yes, I definitely can.' Muhammad Ali, one of the greatest boxers to walk on the face of this planet, was once asked, 'how many sit-ups do you do?' to which he replied, 'I don't count my sit-ups. I only start counting when it starts hurting. When I feel pain, that's when I start counting because that's when it really counts.' So we get a wonderful lesson to work tirelessly and shamelessly if we were to achieve our dreams. Dr. Arnold Schwarzenegger beautifully summed up life's successes in 6 simple rules; Trust yourself, Break some rules, Don't be afraid to fail, Ignore the naysayers, Work like hell, And give something back.

Chapter 9:

Remember The Feeling of Productivity

We all have a big list of ideas, that we want to work on. But we also tend to think that we miss a certain motivation to actually do something. But that is not true in most cases.

The true enemy of one's dreams is the lack of productivity or the feelings to remind you of staying productive like you once were.

Think about it! When you wake up, you pick up that phone, go through your notifications, and get stuck on something. Either consciously or unconsciously, something good or bad gets stuck in our mind, and now our whole day revolves around it.

This is a curse of the modern era. Technology has made us its slave and has taken a big chunk of our creative energies, efforts, and concentration.

Whenever you feel less motivated or have a tendency to get off-rails, remember your most recent productive moments. Try to recall the reasons and motives behind those actions that made you do something useful and productive.

People usually find their productive energies and wishes coming out in odd things. Like a cleaning fetish, some tendency to organize everything, always remaining ahead of everyone, never lose to anyone, or never skip a workout.

Skepticism isn't always bad or worry-some, Not unless you lack a sense of purpose for being skeptical. And this feeling of not being able to get yourself to focus on better things is the flaw leading to failure. It's not the lack of motivation or effort, rather the usage of your energies else-ware.

We often procrastinate either unintentionally or habitually and end up doing trivial activities that don't help us much. Instead, they shape up your routine in a constant cycle of unsuccessful events.

To remove all your distractions. Put away your phone, your laptop, your IPad. Anything that might attract you into spending one more minute and I'll get started.

If you can't give up these things, that's fine. Let's make a game out of it.

For one week, make a deal with yourself. Write three goals for each day, and start making effort for them. Force yourself to not touch your phone till you get at least one of the things done. As soon as you get something done, now, you are allowed to have a bit of distraction to regain some thoughts and perspective.

It's never about perfection, it's always about progress. If you can hold yourself for a little time, with practice you will enter a stage of mind, where you are not reliant on anything but yourself.

Productivity isn't just a set of acts that you perform in a block of time. Productivity is the meaning that we attach to things. Productivity is the mindset that drives your life around a path. Productivity is a choice.

But this feeling of productivity isn't a public garden, rather a hard bet that requires you to make a gutsy call of hardship and stamina.

So get out of your head, Stop thinking about what you need to do, and start doing it.

Chapter 10:

The Goal Is Not The Point

If you ever want to achieve your goals, stop thinking about them. I know this goes against everything anyone has ever said about achieving your goals.

Everyone says that think about one thing and then stick to it. Devote yourself to that one single goal as you are committed to your next breath. Check on your goals over and over again to see if you are still on track or not and you will get there sooner than you think.

What I am proposing is against all the theories that exist behind achieving your goals but wait a minute and listen to me.

The reason behind this opposing theory is that we spend more time concentrating on thinking and panning about our goals. Rather than actually doing something to achieve them.

We think about getting into college. Getting a Bachelor's degree and then getting our Master's degree and so on. So that we can finally decide to appear for an interview that we have dreamed about or to start a business that we are crazy about.

But these are not the requirements for any of them to happen. You can get a degree in whatever discipline you want or not, and can still opt for business. As far as job interviews are concerned, they are not looking for the most educated person for that post. But the most talented and experienced person that suits the role on hand.

So we purposefully spend our life doing things that carry the least importance in actual to that goal.

What we should be doing is to get started with the simplest things and pile upon them as soon as possible. Because life is too short to keep thinking.

Thinking is the easiest way out of our miseries. Staying idol and fantasizing about things coming to reality is the lamest thing to do when you can actually go out and start discovering the opportunities that lie ahead of you.

Your goals are things that are out of your control. You might get them, you might not. But the actions, motivation, and the effort you put behind your goal make the goal a small thing when you actually grab it. Because then you look back and you feel proud of yourself for what you have achieved throughout the journey.

At the end of that journey, you feel happier and content with what you gained within yourself irrespective of the goal. Because you made yourself realize your true potential and your true purpose as an active human being.

Find purpose in the journey for you can't know for sure about what lies ahead. But what you do know is that you can do what you want to do to your own limits. When you come to realize your true potential, the original goal seems to fade away in the background. Because then your effort starts to appear in the foreground.

A goal isn't always meant to be achieved as it might not be good for you in the end or in some other circumstances. But the efforts behind these goals serve as something to look back on and be amazed at.

Chapter 11:

Why Having Lesser Things Actually Makes You Happier

How many of you feel like spending money to acquire more stuff would make you happier because you believe having more things would bring you happiness and life satisfaction?

Now I'm not talking about basic necessities such as food, toiletries, or household appliances that you would actually use on a daily basis for the betterment of your own lives.

I'm talking about a constant need to purchase things as you go shopping at a mall, such as clothes, jackets, ornaments, cups, gadgets, bags, shoes, watches. Or even random stuff that you won't really use or need as you go on various shopping platforms online, especially during huge sale days like black friday or some other major holiday where discounts are abundant and you believe that if you don't buy this now that you are missing out on a great deal.

You might not notice this at the start, but before you know it, your house is starting to feel cluttered as every inch of your house is filled stuff with no place to put them. You might even start going to IKEA to buy shelves and cupboards to house these items in places where you will probably never see or touch them again in the foreseeable future. And they end up hidden there collecting dust.

Not to mention that all these incessant buying has also costed you money over the years.

What was once a clean home with a nice living space has turned into a cramped box of unwanted items that don't bring benefit or betterment to your lives.

How many of you can relate to that? Because that is what I used to do.

Just a few years back, when i wanted to buy clothes i would literally ransack the whole discount section of a particular store and checkout 10s of clothes in one shopping trip. And before i knew it my wardrobe was filled with so many clothes that i had a hard time going through them or deciding what i wanted to wear. And I also realised that i didn't really like most of what i had bought. Which lead to more buying. The same went for my obsession for gadgets. After a year i had so many iPads and iPhones that i did not know what to do with them that costed my thousands of dollars.

When I woke up one day and looked around my house, i realised that i regretted most of the purchases I made and that all these stuff was actually making me very unhappy.

So I did what made sense to me at the time, I started decluttering.

I went through each and every item in my house from my wardrobe to my bedroom, to my study and living room. And with each item held in my hand i asked myself 3 questions: "do i really need this?" "does this make me happy?" and "can someone else make better use of this item?"

And as i started sorting i realised that 70% of my things were stuff that i do not need and will not use. and only 30% of them actually brought me some sort of joy. The most prominent being the clothes i always wore even when i had countless others to choose from.

As I began donating to salvation army and discarding the junk, my house became less and less messy and cramped. And what remained was not only more space, but things that I had an emotional attachment to. Things that brought me a sense of joy when i loooked at them or touched them. The extra space also brought me a sense of peace that there were no hidden junk in cupboards and the space I had could put to better use rather than housing useless things.

This decluttering process was not only therapeutic but necessary for me. For the first time i felt that having lesser things actually made me happier. And That i didnt have to spend my way to achieve happiness. I also realised that what I had already in my house was more than I would ever need and that this is my sacred space that i should only fill with things that are meaningful to me.

What changed for me is that these days when i go shopping, I don't have the urge to spend money on things just because anymore. I end up gravitating towards shops that sells plants, fishes because those are what brings me joy these days. Living things that I have to care for with love and dedication.

This change in wanting lesser things has not only made me happier but also saved me money in the process.

I just want to end off by saying that having more things will never make you happy, but making more friends and being grateful for what you already have can give u the happiness you have been searching for.

Chapter 12:

5 Lessons on Being Wrong

Being wrong isn't as bad as we make it out to be. I have made many mistakes, and I have discovered five major lessons from my experiences.

1. Choices that seem poor in hindsight are an indication of growth, not self-worth or intelligence. When you look back on your choices from a year ago, you should always hope to find a few decisions that seem stupid now because that means you are growing. If you only live in the safety zone where you know you can't mess up, then you'll never unleash your true potential. If you know enough about something to make the optimal decision on the first try, then you're not challenging yourself.

2. Given that your first choice is likely to be wrong, the best thing you can do is get started. The faster you learn from being wrong, the sooner you can discover what is right. Complex situations like relationships or entrepreneurship have to <u>start before you feel ready</u> because no one can be truly ready. The best way to learn is to <u>start practicing</u>.

3. Break down topics that are too big to master into smaller tasks that can be mastered. I can't look at any business and tell you what to do. Entrepreneurship is too big of a topic. But, I can look at any website and tell you how to optimize it for building an email list because that topic is small enough for me to develop some level of expertise. If you want to get better at making accurate first choices, then play in a smaller arena. As Niels Bohr, the Nobel Prize-winning physicist, famously said, "An expert is a person who has made all the mistakes that can be made in a very narrow field."

4. The time to trust your gut is when you have the knowledge or experience to back it up. You can trust yourself to make sharp decisions in areas where you already have proven expertise. For everything else, the only way to discover what works is to adopt a philosophy of experimentation.

5. The fact that failure will happen is not an excuse for expecting to fail. There is no reason to be depressed or give up simply because you will make a few wrong choices. Even more crucial, you must try your best every time because the effort and the practice drive the learning process. They are essential, even if you fail. Realize that no single choice is destined to fail, but that occasional failure is the cost you must pay if you want to be right. Expect to win and play like it from the outset.

Your first choice is rarely the optimal choice. Make it now, stop judging yourself, and start growing.

Chapter 13:

How To Stop Wasting Time

In the inspiring words of Marcia Wider, "It's how we spend our time here, and now, that really matters. If you are fed up with the way you have come to interact with time, change it."

Indeed, time waits for no man. The ticking of the clock should be a startling revelation to you that how precious our time on this earth is. A study conducted at the University of Calgary shows that the ratio of chronic procrastination has increased from 5% in 1978 to 26% in 2007. In other words, you don't need more time. You have to do MORE with the time you already have. Stop wasting your time on the things that don't really matter. Do you realize how many seconds and minutes and hours do we waste every day on stuff that doesn't even let us come close to reaching our goals? If you've ever come to ask yourself, "where does the time go?" then maybe you should re-think how and on what you're spending your time.

"A man who dares to waste one hour has not discovered the value of time." Charles Darwin. There are only as many as 24 hours in a day, and you've got to make sure that each of them counts for something. There's a date on the left side of the tombstone, that's the date on which you were born. When you die, another date is engraved on the right side of your tombstone, but that dash, that line that you see in the middle of both these dates, decides how much you left your mark on other people's lives as well as your own, how much you were able to impact others, that dash represents how you lived your life in the timeframe that you were given.

We all get the same amount of time. A homeless person or a beggar that wanders here and there all day brings the same amount of time as the most successful businessman. It's what we do with that time, how we presume the ticking of the clock that genuinely matters. Life flickers by us in the blink of an eye. And what do we do about that? We only give excuses and justifications. "I don't have time to go to the gym, and maybe I'll start tomorrow. I'll start studying tomorrow; one day of taking a break won't make a difference" NO! It would make all the difference in the world. Stop fearing and pitying yourself and get up. Stop wasting your time because it's a depreciating asset, and you won't get any of it back.

You have to take the first step. You can't just live your life fearing the challenges and efforts you have to put in to get somewhere higher in life. Procrastinating, watching your favorite TV show adds up to so much time, even for an hour each day. And that time is nothing but wasted. Imagine the knowledge you can gain in that one hour of each day, imagine the work that you could do, the language that you can learn, the instrument that you can learn to play. So start investing your time into something productive rather than just lying here making defenses.

"Newton's first law of productivity" states that objects at rest tend to stay at rest until they're acted upon. That book on your shelf isn't going to read itself, those weights in the gym aren't going to move by themselves, that long due essay isn't going to write itself, YOU. HAVE. TO. DO. IT! And you have to do it now. Don't wait for another hour or another day or another week; you have to take that leap of faith; you have to take that risk. Specify your days, prioritize your to-do list, eliminate all the distractions. Nothing will make you happier than knowing that you're making progress towards becoming a better version of yourself. Take breaks, but get yourself back up to your goals. Don't waste your time! "Whatever you want to do, do it now! There are only so many tomorrow's." – Pope Paul VI.

FOCUS! You should be terrified of living a life on the sidelines. Of not achieving anything whether you're 6, 16, or 60. Of doing nothing and watching the time passes by, of not making any progress and not being able to come closer to your dreams, your goals. Stop being stagnant! Start working towards your passion, your dreams, your aspirations. The separator between the people that win and lose is what we do with that time, with those seconds that we get in a day. Start working towards self-mastery, and you will begin to see the difference in all the dimensions of your life. So concentrate on developing yourself because if you don't, I guarantee you that you will make a settlement, and most people have, and most of us already have. The proper function of a man is to live, not just only to exist. We shall not waste our days trying to prolong them only, but we shall use our time effectively.

Time is free, but it's also priceless. It's perhaps the most essential commodity in this world. Once you've lost it, you can never get it back. Look back and see how many hours and days and years have you wasted doing absolutely nothing? Don't shy up from the tough things. We can't make excuses and then expect to be successful at the same time. We have to get up every day and make sure we don't quit ourselves, our goals, our dreams, our passions. Make mistakes, make them thousand times over, but make sure you learn something from every single one of them. We can't travel back to time and change the past. So don't dwell on the things that happened yesterday or months ago. Start working towards your future. We only have a limited time here on earth. It's better to spend time waiting for the opportunity to take action than miss the chance.

"Determine never to be idle. No person will have occasion to complain of the want of time who never loses any. It is wonderful how much can be done if we are always doing." - Thomas Jefferson.

Chapter 14:

Discovering Your Strengths and Weaknesses

Today we're going to talk about a very simple yet important topic that hopefully brings about some self discovery about who you really are. By the end of this video i wish to help you find out what areas you are weak at so that maybe you could work on those, and what your strengths are so that you can play to them and lean into them more for greater results in your career and life in general.

We should all learn to accept our flaws as much as we embrace our strengths. And we have to remember that each of us are unique and we excel in different areas. Some of us are more artistic, some visionary, some analytical, some hardworking, some lazy, what matters is that we make these qualities work for us in our own special way.

Let's start by identifying your weaknesses. For those of you that have watched enough of my videos, you would know that i encourage all of you to take a pen to write things down. So lets go through this exercise real quick. Think of a few things that people have told you that you needed to work on, be it from your Teachers, your friends, your family, or whoever it may be.

How many of these weaknesses would you rate as significantly important that it would affect your life in a drastic way if you did not rectify it? I want you to put them at the top of your list. Next spend some time to reflect and look in the mirror. Be honest with yourself and identify the areas about yourself that you know needs some work.

Now I want you to take some time to identity your strengths. Repeat the process from above, what are the things people have told you about yourself that highlighted certain qualities about you? Whether that you're very outgoing, friendly, a great singer, a good team player, very diligent. I want you to write as many of these down as you can. No matter how big or small these strengths are, I want you to write down as many as you can.

Now I want you to also place your 3 biggest strengths at the top of the list. As I believe these are the qualities that best represent who you are as a person.

Now that you've got these 2 lists. I want you to compare them. Which list is longer? the one with strengths or weaknesses? If you have more weaknesses, that's okay, it just means that there is more room for improvement. If you have more strengths, thats good.

What we are going to do with this list now is to now make it a mission to improve our weaknesses and play heavily into our strengths for the foreseeable future. You see, our strengths are strengths for a reason, we are simply naturally good at it. Whether it be through genetics, or our personalities, or the way we have been influenced by the world. We should all try to showcase our strengths as much as we can. It is hard for me to say exactly what that is, but I believe that you will know how you maximise the use of your talent. Whether it be serving others, performing for others, or even doing specific focused tasks. Simply do more of it. Put yourself in more situations where you can practice these strengths. And keep building on it. It will take little effort but yield tremendous results.

As for your weaknesses, I want you to spend some time on the top 3 that you have listed so far. As these could be the areas that have been holding you back the most. Making improvements in these areas could be the breakthrough that you need to become a much better person and could see you achieving a greater level success than if you had just left them alone.

I challenge each and everyone of you to continually play to your strengths, sharpening them until they are sharp as a knife, while working on smoothening the rough edges of your weaknesses. So that they may balance out your best qualities.

Chapter 15:

Seven Habits That Drain Your Energy

We own some bad habits to the point that we cannot see past them. They are a veil in front of our eyes and a hindrance to achieving our purpose. Most disappointing of all is that we may not even be aware of these habits until someone else calls them out to our attention.

Here are the seven most common habits that drain your energy.

1. Addiction

It is the most common subconscious habit that most people face. Addiction is not limited to drug and substance abuse. It includes the minor overlooked habits in modern lifestyle – phone use addiction and addiction to the internet.

When one is addicted to something or someone, they tend not to care about anything else except their obsession. Without their object or person of interest, their lives are literally on hold. They idolize their interests and sometimes almost at the point of worship.

The power of addiction should not be underestimated. It makes a person irrational and unreasonable to the point of draining you of your energy, time, and resources whilst chasing the wind. To an addict, the whole world is against him. He is at war with anything and anyone that becomes an obstacle. Addiction turns good people into thieves, beggars, and cons. However, not all hope is lost. Even great addicts are redeemable. It begins with self-realization followed by a personal decision to start over and reform. Under the right tutelage, you can redeem yourself from those chronic addictive habits that drain your energy and potential.

2. Idleness

Ironically, idleness can drain your energy. You may be asking how it is even possible to engage in nothing and still lose something. The absence of evidence is not the evidence of absence (read that again). You have more to lose than gain when you are idle. An idle mind is the devil's workshop.

Idleness completely destroys any potential in a person. It robs you of the ability to channel your energy in the right direction rendering you unproductive. Some say that idleness is better than engaging in crime or other vices, but truth is that idle minds are fertile grounds for evil plans. One cannot realize his true potential in a state of idleness.

It takes so little to drain off one's energy more than it takes to replenish used energy. Idleness is a catalyst for the former. Strive to fight idleness tooth and nail. To ward off bad luck, unproductiveness and ineffectiveness, always engage your mind in some activity. Practice makes perfect, and this extends to the use of the mind. Continually engaging in progressive acts will sharpen your wit and intelligence. This is not achievable in an idle state.

3. Ignorance

Ignorance is a lack of knowledge. From a point of ignorance, your vision is veiled. You become blind to great opportunities ahead and regrettably, drains one's energy and ability to maximize untapped potential.

Ignorance is a hindrance to excellence. In the words of Aristotle, Excellence is not an act but a habit. So is ignorance since lack of it brings excellence. When the habit of ignorance takes root in a person, doom is inevitable. It will drain your energy to uphold knowledge completely and seal your fatal end.

Sovereign governments worldwide are fighting ignorance in their population. Lack of formal education is unheard and every measure is in place to combat ignorance. It begins with a personal decision to shun it. Be informed of relevant occurrences to guard against belief and the spread of unfounded rumors. Rumormongering is not a portion of strong-willed people.

4. Work Holism

It is one of the biggest problems facing most modern people. They work throughout thinking that it will make them forget their problems. This is entirely false. The opposite is true. Work holism achieves the unintended. It compiles your problems without solving any of them.

The best way to solve problems is to address them exhaustively. Finding escape channels like overworking oneself solves nothing. Instead, it is a sign of timidity and cowardice. Work holism drains your energy especially if you are in formal employment. The input in your work goes beyond your contribution to your life. It is a shame that is the point many people have reached.

Like any other bad habit that people develop over time, one can overcome work holism. First, own up to your problems and walk the journey of addressing them one at a time. You may engage a mentor or an authority to help you overcome this vice.

5. Procrastination

Procrastination is not a habit of successful people. It is also one of the biggest challenges facing most modern people. Why do it later when you can do it now? In response to this question, several invalid reasons come up.

It may be habitual laziness or a bad culture of shelving actions for an unspecified later time but procrastination is the reason why most people have not exploited their full potential. Their ability lies idle and their energy drained by their fruitless habits.

To cure procrastination, unlearn your old habits. Get rid of how you used to do things in the past and begin acting on matters as soon as it is possible. There is a caveat. Do not rush into action solely because you do not want to procrastinate. Two wrongs do not make a right. Be sober as you fight procrastination.

6. Underestimating Your Competitors

A wise once said, "Keep your friends close, and your enemies closer." The truth in this is so significant. When you underestimate your competitors, you do not leash your full potential. You hold back what could have given you an edge over them.

When defeat knocks on your door, it drains your morale and energy. Psychological distress ensues because you did not take the challenge seriously. When you listen to many stories of hopelessness, the common denominator is drained energy after a defeat brought by underestimating competitors.

7. Unresolved Family Conflicts

We may be a product of circumstances in such a setting. However, habitual conflicts in families make us normalize the vices we ought to shun. A family is the building block of a society. Broken families have the potential to drain one's energy and potential. A child's potential is unrealized in a broken family. They grow up seeing themselves as failures. We have little control of our backgrounds. Nevertheless, we can steer our lives towards the path of our desire as we mature. To remedy the same, we learn from our experiences not to raise our generation in the paths we went through.

Chapter 16:

Discovering Your Purpose

If you guys don't already know, this is one of the topics that I really love talking about. And I never get tired of it. Having a purpose is something that I always believe everyone should have. Having a purpose to live, to breathe, to get up each day, I believe that without purpose, there is no point to life.

So today we're going to talk about how to discover your purpose, and why you should make it a point to find one if you didn't already start looking.

So what is purpose exactly. A purpose is a reason to do something. Is to have something else greater than ourselves to work for. You see, I believe if we are only focused on ourselves, instead of others, we will not be able to be truly happy in life. Feeding our own self interests does not bring us joy as one might think. After living the life that I had, I realized that true happiness only comes when you bring joy to someone else's life. Whether it be helping others professionally or out of selflessness, this happiness will radiate and reflect back to us from someone else who is appreciative of your efforts.

On some level, we can look into ourselves to be happy. For example being grateful for life, loving ourselves, and all that good stuff. Yes keep doing those things. But there is a whole other dimension if we devote our time and energy into helping others once we have already conquered ourselves. If you look at many of the most successful people on the planet, after they have acquired an immense amount of wealth, many of them look to passion projects or even philanthropy where they can give back to the community when having more money doesn't do anything for them anymore. If you look at Elon Musk and Jeff Bezos, these two have a greater purpose which is their space projects. Where they visualise humans being able to move out of Earth one day where civilisation is able to expand. Or Bill Gates and Warren Buffet, who have pledged to give billions of their money away for philanthropic work, to help the less fortunate and to fund organisations that work towards finding cures to diseases.

Now for us mere mortals, we don't need to think so big. Our purpose need not be so extravagant. It can be as simple as having a purpose to provide for your loved one, to work hard to bring your family members of holidays and travel, or to bring joy to your elderly relatives by organising activities for them to do. There is no purpose that is too big or too small.

Your purpose could be helping others find a beautiful home, doing charitable work, or even feeding and providing for your growing family.

As humans, we will automatically work harder if we have a clear and defined purpose. We have a reason to get up each day, to go to work, to earn that paycheck, so that we can spend it on things and people, even ourselves at times. Without a purpose, we struggle to find meaning in the work that we do. We struggle to see the big picture and we find that we have no reason to work so hard, or even at all. And we struggle to find life worth living.

This revelation came to me when I started seeing my work as helping some other person in a meaningful way. Where my work was not just about making money to buy nice things, but to be able to impact someone else's life in a positive way. That became my purpose. To see them learn something new, and to bring a joy and smile to their faces. That thought that I was contributing something useful to someone made me smile more than money ever could. Yes money can help you live a comfortable life, but helping others can go a much farther way into giving your life true purpose.

So I challenge each and everyone of you to find a purpose in everything that you do, and if you struggle to find one, start by making the goal to help others a priority. Think of the difference you can make to others and that could very well be your purpose in life as well.

Chapter 17:

Five Habits That Make You Age Faster

We will all get old one day. A day is coming when we will not have the youthful energy we presently enjoy. Everyone desires that this day should never come or rather come very late in our lifetime. Nevertheless, it is an inevitable occurrence. We can only delay it.

Here are five habits that make you age faster:

1. Unforgiveness

Unforgiveness is like hiding fire expecting that no one will notice. Eventually, the smoke will give you away. It arises when one deeply wrongs us leaving a trail of hurt and agony that cannot easily be forgotten. The offended party will never forget what was committed against him/her. Anytime he/she sees the other person, the bad memory is re-kindled.

It is unhealthy to hold on to such bad memories. They cause mental and emotional trauma. They cause and affect your health. When your health is affected due to your unforgiveness, you bear full consequences and can only blame yourself. However subtle it may seem, unforgiveness is responsible for the fast aging of many people who harbor it.

The offender could probably have even forgotten about it and moved on with his/her life. The victim is the one who will be left bearing the brunt of the hurt. Stress will manifest on your face in the form of contortions making you appear aged than you are. Choose forgiveness always and you will lead a happier youthful life.

2. Bitterness

Bitterness is an aftermath of unforgiveness. It is a very strong emotion that succeeds unforgiveness. Regardless that it springs forth from within, bitterness manifests on the face over time. The glory on the face of a joyous person is absent on that of a bitter person.

Ever asked yourself how people can judge someone's age bracket? The youthful glamour disappears on the face of a bitter person. Some elderly people appear very youthful. The reason is that they live a bitter-free life. Such a type of lifestyle guarantees youthfulness.

Strive to be youthful and live a fulfilling life by keeping bitterness at bay. Entertaining it will increase the rate at which you age and may succumb to old-age diseases while still at a very young age.

3. Lack of Physical Exercise

Physical exercise is an important part of the human routine. It is not reserved for sports people only but everyone needs it to grow healthy. So important is exercise that it is incorporated in the education curriculum for students to observe.

Physical exercises help one become healthy and look youthful. It burns excess calories in our body and unblocks blood vessels thus increasing the efficiency of blood flow and body metabolism. Excess water, salts, and toxins are expelled from our bodies when we sweat after intense exercise.

The lack of physical exercise makes our bodies stiff and they become a fertile ground for lifestyle diseases like high blood pressure. Conversely, exercises improve our body shape and sizes by shedding extra weight. This healthy lifestyle brought by regular exercises will enable us to live a long healthy disease-free life.

4. Poor Dieting

Dieting serves several purposes but the chief benefit of a proper dieting habit is that it gives the body important nutrients and shields it from excesses caused by human bias. Proper dieting will make you eat nutritive food that you may even not like. The benefits of nutritive meals outweigh your tastes and preferences.

Poor dieting is taking meals without considering their nutritive value or repetitively eating a meal because you love it. This habit makes you caution less with what you eat. You will ingest excess oily and fatty foods which will harm the healthy bacteria that live in your gut. It goes further to affect your heart health and immune response to diseases.

These factors directly affect the rate at which you age. Greasy foods will manifest in your skin and alter your appearance. It may also cause acne on your face. To reduce your aging rate, improve your dieting habit and supply the body with the right nutrients.

5. Lack Of A Skincare Routine

As much as the skin is affected by the type of meals we take, a healthy skin care routine plays a major role in maintaining youthful skin. There are many celebrities globally who look younger than their age and this has a lot to do with their skincare routine.

It varies from one person to another but the fundamentals are constant - washing your face with plenty of clean water in the morning and evening. This is to remove dirt and dead cells from the skin. When one does not take care of his/her skin, aging creeps in. The face is the most visible part of the human body and it requires maximum care.

Failure to have an efficient skincare routine will entertain old age - the last item on our wish list.

Since we are now enlightened about habits that will make us age faster, the onus is on us to fight them and remain youthful.

Chapter 18:

The Magic of Journaling

Today we're going to talk about the power of journaling, and why you should start making it as part of your daily habit starting today.

Everyday, every second of our lives, we are bombarded with things coming at our way. From our colleagues, our bosses, to our friends, families, relationships, and most importantly, ourselves. Life gets hectic and crazy sometimes. We have a million things racing through our minds and we don't have the time or place to let it all out so we keep it bottled up inside.

This creates a backlog of emotions, feelings, things, that we leave undealt with. We start to miss the little details along the way, or our mood gets affected because we can't seem to get rid of the negativity festering up inside of us. If we don't have anyone readily available to talk to us, these feelings that have been building inside of us could end up spilling over and affecting our performance at the workplace, at home, whatever it may be.

We are not able to perform these roles at home or at work effectively as a result. This is where the power of journaling comes into play.

Journaling is such an important tool for us to put into paper or into words every single emotion that we are feeling. Every thought that we are thinking. And this works sort of like a cleanse. We are cleansing, decluttering, and unpacking all the things that are jumbled up in our head. By writing these feelings down, we are not only able to keep a clear head, but it also gives us a reference point to come back to if there are any unresolved problems that we feel we need to work on at a later date.

Journaling has worked wonders for me. I've never thought it to be a habit work incorporating into my life because i thought hey, it's another thing for me to do on top of my already hectic day. I don't have time for this. Basically giving 1001 reasons not to do it.

But I came across this life coach that described the wonders of journaling as I am describing to you right now. And I thought. Why not just give it a try.

I did. And it changed my life.

I never realized how powerful journaling could actually be in transforming my state of mind and to always keep me grounded and focused. Everytime I felt that i was distracted, had something I couldn't work through in my mind, I would pick up my ipad and start typing it down in a journal app.

With technology, it has made journaling a much more enjoyable experience for me and one that i can simply do on the fly, anywhere, anytime. I didn't have to fumble around to find my pen and book, i just opened up the app and started typing away every single feeling and thought.

Journaling helped me see the big picture. It helped me become more aware of the things that are working for me and things that aren't. I was able to focus more on the areas that were bringing more joy in my life and to eliminate the situations and activities that were draining me of my energy and spirit.

Journaling can be anything you want it to be. There are no fixed rules as to how you must journal. Just write whatever comes to your mind. You will be surprised by how much you can learn from yourself. Many a times we forget that we are our best teacher. Other people can't learn our lessons for us, only we can.

So next time you feel sluggish, depressed, unhappy, or even ecstatic and over the moon, write down how and why you got to that place. No judgement, no berating yourself, just pouring your heart and soul onto a piece of paper or into a journaling app. I'll be looking forward to hearing of your transformation from the power of journaling.

Chapter 19:

There's No Time for Regrets

Regret. Guilt. Shame.

These are three of the darkest emotions any human will ever experience. We all feel these things at different points in our lives, especially after making a "bad" decision. There are certain situations some of us would rewind (or delete) if we could. The reality is, however, there is an infinite number of reasons we should never regret any of the decisions we make in our lives.

Here are 7 of them:

1. Every decision allows you to take credit for creating your own life.

Decisions are not always the result of thoughtful contemplation. Some of them are made on impulse alone. Regardless of the decision, when you made it, it was something you wanted, or you would not have done it (unless someone was pointing a gun at your head). Be willing to own the decisions you make. Be accountable for them. Take responsibility and accept them.

2. By making any decision involving your heart, you have the chance to create more love in the world by spreading yours.

Your love is a gift.

Once you decide to love, do it without reservation. By fully giving of yourself, you expand your ability to express and receive love. You have added to the goodness of our universe by revealing your heart to it.

3. By experiencing the disappointment that might come with a decision's outcome, you can propel yourself to a new level of emotional evolution.

You aren't doing yourself any favors when you try to save yourself from disappointment. Disappointment provides you with an opportunity to redefine your experiences in life. By refining your reframing skills, you increase your resilience.

4. "Bad" decisions are your opportunity to master the art of self-forgiveness.

When you make a "bad" decision, *you* are the person who is usually the hardest on yourself. Before you can accept the consequences of your decision and move on, you must forgive yourself. You won't always make perfect choices in your life. Acknowledge the beauty in your human imperfection, then move forward and on.

5. Because of the occasional misstep, you enable yourself to live a Technicolor life.

Anger. Joy. Sadness.

These emotions add pigment to your life. Without these things, you would feel soulless. Your life would be black and white.

Make your decisions with gusto. Breathe with fire. You are here to live in color.

6. Your ability to make a decision is an opportunity to exercise the freedom that is your birthright.

How would you feel if you had no say in those decisions concerning your life? Would you feel powerless? Restricted? Suffocated. Now, focus on what it feels like to make the decisions you want to make. What do you feel? Freedom? Liberty? Independence?

What feelings do you *want* to feel? Freedom. Liberty. Independence. As luck would have it, the freedom you want is yours. Be thankful for it in every decision you make, "good" or "bad."

7. When you decide to result in ugly aftermath, you refine what you *do* want in your life.

It's often impossible to know what you want until you experience what you don't want. With every decision, you will experience consequences. Use those outcomes as a jumping-off point to something different (and better) in your future.

Chapter 20:

Never Giving Up

Today I'm going to talk about a topic that I feel very inspired to share. In recent times, never giving up has helped me to push through the initial failures that I had experienced when it came to my career which I later found traction in. I hope that the story today will inspire you also do the same.

It Is all too easy for us to give up when the going gets tough. Starting something new is always much easier but sticking through it and grinding through all the problems that you will most certainly face, is the greater challenge on the road to success that many of us are not willing to put ourselves through.

In recent years, I have had many occasions that it was my persistence that actually yielded the fruits of my labour 2-3 years after I had begun the journey. Success was not found immediately.

A few years ago, I began my online career to make money and I found a new business that I was interested in. I invested time and money into it and found some success in the beginning. I gave up all prior aspirations to pursue a traditional career to embark on this journey and I had nothing to lose.

However after 2 years pouring my heart and soul in this venture, I faced a tough reality when something happened to my business and I lost everything. I lost my sole stream of income and I felt absolutely lost, not to mention crushed that all my time had literally gone up in smoke. I started to doubt myself and question why I even bothered embarking on this path in the first place. I really did not know what to do and had no Plan B. I spent the next few months wandering about trying to figure out what's next. At one point I did feel like giving up and going back to finding a regular job despite knowing that that is something I really did not want to do.

After months of exploring, I decided that I would give my first venture another go. I created a new account and began the journey again, from scratch. I faced many obstacles that were not there before and the struggle was terribly real. I felt pressure from myself to make it work because I felt that there was nothing I was really good at. I needed to prove to myself that I wasn't a failure and that fire lit up inside me to be successful at it at all cost.

To put it simply, eventually my persistence did pay off and I managed to build back some of the income stream that I had lost with new strategies that I had employed. What I only realised much later was that it was actually my experience having been in the business for two years prior that helped me navigate this new strategy much quicker. Everything was done at lightning speed despite the obstacles and I was astounded by the pace in which it picked up. It was in that moment that I understood the principle of never giving up. Because if I had, I would have literally flushed away all the time and energy I had invested earlier in the business down the toilet. It was my attitude of never giving up, and learning from my mistakes that got me through the second time around.

Another story that I want to share about never giving up is something much simpler, and it had to Do with something that happened around the house.

In a random event, somehow my door got jammed by an appliance around the house. And no matter how hard I tried to push it simply wouldn't budge. After cracking my head for hours, together with my parents, we still couldn't figure out how to get the door to open no matter how many things we tried. At one point my dad decided that the only way was to break down the door. However the persistence in me didn't want to give up. I found a strategy that could possibly work, involving a knife, and long story short I managed to get the door to open with a great deal of strength. In that moment I felt like the king of the world. Never giving up and persisting felt like the greatest feeling on Earth. And it got me fired up to want to apply this same persistence to all aspects of my life.

It was with these joint experiences along with many others that gave me the conviction that solidified the principle that I have been hearing from gurus every single day about never giving up. That only when you had given up have you truly failed. And I believe every single one of those words today.

So I challenge each and everyone of you today to try this out for yourself. To go back to something you have decided that you had called quits on and to give it one more try. Use your expertise, use your experience, learn from your mistakes of what went wrong before, modify the new plan, and try again. You might be surprised at the outcome. Never ever give up because it's never really over until you have decided to quit.

Chapter 21:

Dealing With Worries

Everyone worries from time to time. Too much worry can be bad as it leaves us feeling tense and anxious. Even though we might say to ourselves and others – "Stop worrying. It's pointless. It won't do any good" – there is something about worrying that makes it hard to stop. This is because worry can be helpful.

Useful worry prompts action. All other worry is pointless.

• Worry is useful if it makes you pay attention

Worrying about the weather cannot stop it raining on your washing; however, if you watch the sky and act to bring in your washing when it rains, being aware that it will have helped.

• Worry is useful, provided it is turned into a plan for action

For example, worrying that your electricity might get cut off might lead you to act to pay your bill on time. Once the bill has been paid, the worrying would stop, and you would feel better.

• Worry is useful if it helps you be better prepared

Worry may help you think about "what you could do if...," or "what would happen if...". Worrying "what would happen if my house was burgled" could make you act to take out house insurance and lock your front door when you go out.

Worry without action does nothing

I worry on its own did something then we could worry all day to increase our bank balance. On the other hand taking action such as selling something, working more hours, or spending less will directly affect our bank balance.

Is it worth worrying about?

Four things are not worth worrying about, but that account for many of our worries: the unimportant, the unlikely, the uncertain, and the uncontrollable. Ban these from your life, and you will worry less.

The Unimportant

It is easy to fill your life with worries about little things. When you find yourself worrying, start to question yourself instead. Ask yourself, "How important is the thing that I am worried about?"

Here are three points to help you answer this question.

1. **The five-year rule**: Ask yourself: "will this matter in 5 years?" This is a way of looking at your worry from a long-term point of view. View your worries differently: will this still be a concern in a week, a month, or a year?

2. **The measuring rod:** Ask yourself: "Where, on a scale of bad experiences, is the thing I'm worried about?" Think about a very

bad experience you have had. How does your current worry feel when compared with this?

3. **The calculator:** Ask yourself: "How much worry is this worth?" We only have a certain amount of time and energy. Make sure you do not spend more worry on your problem than it is worth. You need your time and energy for more important things. Maybe some time you would have spent worrying could be used for doing something.

Chapter 22:

Enjoying The Simple Things

Today we're going to talk about a topic that might sound cheesy, but trust me it's worth taking a closer look at. And that is how we should strive to enjoy the simple things in life.

Many of us think we need a jam packed schedule for the week, month, or year, to tell us that we are leading a very productive and purposeful life. We find ways to fill our time with a hundred different activities. Going to this event, that event, never slowing down. And we find ourselves maybe slightly burnt out by the end of it.

We forget that sometimes simplicity is better than complication. Have you sat down with your family for a simple lunch meal lately? You don't have to talk, you just have to be in each other's company and enjoying the food that is being served in front of you.

I found myself appreciating these moments more than I did running around to activities thinking that I needed something big to be worth my time. I found sitting next to my family on the couch watching my own shows while they watch theirs very rewarding. I found eating alone at my favourite restaurant while watching my favourite sitcom to be equally as enjoyable as hanging out with a group of 10 friends. I also found myself richly enjoying a long warm shower every morning and evening. It is the highlights of my day.

My point is that we need to start looking at the small things we can do each day that will bring us joy. Things that are within our control. Things that we know can hardly go wrong. This will provide some stability to gain some pleasure from. The little nuggets in the day that will not be determined by external factors such as the weather, friends bailing on us, or irritating customers.

When we focus on the little things, we make life that much better to live through.

Chapter 23:

Five Habits of Good Speech Delivery

Speech delivery is a hot topic amongst many people with opinions divided on what to or what not to do. Everyone has their struggle in speech delivery; some are shy, others are bold but lack the material content to deliver while another group cannot hold a coherent conversation altogether with strangers.

Here are five fundamental habits of good speech delivery:

1. Understand Your Audience

Whenever given the chance to address an audience, it is imperative to understand the demographic constitution of your audience. Their age, social and political class contributes heavily to how they will perceive your speech. The manner one can deliver a speech to a graduation class at a university is entirely different from how the same speech can be given to entrepreneurs considering the mindset and life priorities of these two groups. When you have a thorough understanding of your audience, your art of public speaking and speech delivery will improve because your audience will relate well.

2. Read The Mood and Setting of Your Audience

The diction and language of your speech are variables of the prevailing mood of the audience. How can you relate with them if you are blind to their present mood (excitement or somberness) or the setting (high or low temperatures)? The wearer of a shoe knows where it pinches. As a speaker, you should be flexible to allow your audience to follow your speech in their most comfortable state. If the weather is hot, allow them to open windows and air ventilation. If they are in a bad mood, make them understand that you feel their plight. Be the bigger person in the room and accommodate everyone. It will earn you respect and your speech will be well received.

3. Understand the Theme of The Speech

This is the core subject matter of the speech. Every speech aims to pass a specific message to its recipients. Under no circumstances should the theme be lost to any other interest. If it does, the speech would be meaningless and a waste of time. The onus is upon the deliverer of the speech to stick to the theme and neither alter nor dilute the message therein. He/she should first understand it to be able to convey the same to the audience. The speaker should not have any malice or prejudice to any section of the audience. They should have clean hands. It is paramount to understand that the audience is not ignorant of the theme of the speech. When you disappoint their expectations, you would have lost their participation and some of them may leave the meeting in progress. The chance to deliver a speech does not render the rest of the audience is inferior to the speaker.

4. Be Bold

Boldness is the courage to speak fearlessly without mincing your words. Bold speakers are rare to come by and when they do, their audience becomes thrilled by their exuberance of knowledge. The content of a speech could be great but when a coward delivers it, the theme is lost. Boldness captures the attention of the audience. They expect the best from a bold speaker. The best orators of our time speak so powerfully that one cannot ignore them. The 44th president of the United States is a perfect example of how he boldly delivered his speeches and commanded respect across the globe. A bold speaker does not bore his/her audience and they are more likely to remember a speech that they delivered compared to those of timid speakers. Fortune favors the bold.

5.   Engage Your Audience

It is important to bring onboard your audience when you are delivering a speech. They will feel included and it will be more of a conversation than a talk down. When an audience actively participates in the delivery of a speech, it is more likely they will remember it. As a speaker, maintain eye contact with the audience. This will create a connection with them and remove the notion that you are afraid of them. From time to time in your speech, rope them in to answer a relatable question. An audience expectant of engagement from its speaker will be more attentive.   A speech is not a monologue. It is an interaction between the speaker and his/her audience. When a speaker monopolizes a speech, it becomes boring and easily forgettable. It may further come out as a show-off rather than a genuine speech of a particular theme.

These are the five key habits if you want to maximize the delivery of your speech.

Chapter 24:

How to stop procrastinating:

Procrastination; perhaps the most used word of our generation. Procrastination can range from a minor issue that hurts your productivity or a significant issue that's preventing you from achieving your goals. You feel powerless, and you feel hopeless; you feel de-motivated, De-strategized, even guilty and ashamed, but all in vain.

Let me in all of you on a secret of life, the need to avoid pain and the desire to gain pleasure. That is what we consider the two driving forces of life. Repeat this mantra till it gets in the back of your head. And if you don't take control over these two forces, they'll take control over you and your entire life. The need to avoid pain is what gets us into procrastinating. We aren't willing to step out of our comfort zone, be uncomfortable, fear the pain of spending our energies, fear failure, embarrassment, and rejection. We don't simply procrastinate because there's no other choice; we procrastinate because whatever it is, we don't consider it essential to us. It's not that something meaningful for us or urgent to us, and when something doesn't feel binding to us, we tend to put it off. We link to link a lot of pain to not taking action. But what if we reversed the roles? What if we start to connect not taking action to be more painful than taking action. We have to change our perspective. See that the long-term losses of not taking action are 1000x more painful than the short-term losses of taking those actions.

Stop focusing on the short-term pain of spending your time, energy, and emotions on the tasks at hand. START focusing on the long-term pain that comes when you'll realize you're not even close to the goals you were meant to achieve.

Stop your desire to gain pleasure from the unnecessary and unimportant stuff. You would rather skip your workout to watch a movie instead. You're focusing on the pleasure, the meaningless short-term craving that'll do you no good. Imagine the pleasure we'd gain if we actually did that workout. Stop making excuses for procrastinating. Start owning up to yourself, your tasks, your goals. Set a purpose in your life and start working tirelessly towards it. Take breaks but don't lose your focus!

If you're in school and you're not getting the grades that you want, and still you're not doing anything about it, then maybe it's not a priority for you. But how do we make it meaningful? How do we make it purposeful? You need to find that motivation to get yourself going. And I promise you once you find that purpose, you'll get up early in the morning, and you'll start working to make your dreams come true.

Don't just talk about it, be about it! You were willing to graduate this year, you were willing to go to the gym and change your physique, you were willing to write that book, but what happened? You didn't make them a priority, and you eventually got tired of talking. Take a deep breath and allow yourself to make the last excuse there is that's stopping you from whatever it is that you're supposed to do. I don't have enough money; I don't write well, I don't sing well, I don't have enough knowledge, that's it. That's the last excuse you're going to make and get it over with. Aren't you tired of feeling defeated? Aren't you tired of getting beat? Aren't you tired of saying "I'll get it done soon" over and over again? To all the procrastinators, YOU. STILL. HAVE. PLENTY. OF. TIME. Don't quit, don't give up, don't just lay there doing nothing; you can make it happen. But not with that procrastinating. Set up a goal, tear it into manageable pieces, stop talking about the things you were going to do, and start doing them for real!

It's not too late for anything. There might be some signs that'll show you that you need to rest. Take them. Take the time you need to get back on track. But don't give up on the immediate gratification. Don't listen to that little voice in your head. Get out of bed, lift those weights, start working on that project, climb that mountain. You're the only person that's stopping you from achieving your goals, your dreams. With long-term success, either you're going to kick the hell out of life, or life's going to kick the hell out of you; whichever of that happens the most will become your reality. We're the master of our fates, the ambassador of our ambitions; why waste our time and lives away into doing something that won't even matter to us in a few years? Why not work towards something that will touch people, inspire them, give them hope.

I'll do it in the next hour, I'll do it the next day, I'll do it the next week, and before you know, you're dragging it to the next month or even next year. And that's the pain of life punching you in the face. The regrets of missing opportunities will eventually catch up to you. Every day you get a chance to either make the most out of life or sit on the sidelines taking the crumbles which people are leaving behind. Take what you want or settle for what's left! That's your choice.

You have to push yourself long past the point of boredom. Boredom is your worst enemy. It kills more people in the pursuit of success than anything or anyone will ever destroy. Your life just doesn't stop accidentally. It's a series of actions that you either initiate or don't initiate. Some people have already made their big decisions today, after waking up. While some, they're still dwelling on the things that don't matter. They're afraid of self-evaluation, thus wasting their time. So focus on yourself, focus on what you're doing with your time, have clarity on what you're trying to achieve. Build into what you're trying to accomplish. Between where you are and where you want to go, there's a skill set that you have to master. There's a gap that's asking for your hard work. So pay the price for what you want to become.

Chapter 25:

Trust The Process

Today we're going to talk about the power of having faith that things will work out for you even though you can't see the end in sight just yet. And why you need to simply trust in the process in all the things that you do.

Fear is something that we all have. We fear that if we quit our jobs to pursue our passions, that we may not be able to feed ourselves if our dreams do not work out. We fear that if we embark on a new business venture, that it might fail and we would have incurred financial and professional setbacks.

All this is borne out of the fear of the unknown. The truth is that we really do not know what can or will happen. We may try to imagine in our heads as much as we can, but we can never really know until we try and experienced it for ourselves.

The only way to overcome the fear of the unknown is to take small steps, one day at a time. We will, to the best of our ability, execute the plan that we have set for ourselves. And the rest we leave it up to the confidence that our actions will lead to results.

If problems arise, we deal with it there and then. We put out fires, we implement updated strategies, and we keep going. We keep going until we have exhausted all avenues. Until there is no more roads for us to travel, no more paths for us to create. That is the best thing that we can do.

If we constantly focus on the fear, we will never go anywhere. If we constantly worry about the future, we will never be happy with the present. If we dwell on our past failures, we will be a victim of our own shortcomings. We will not grow, we will not learn, we will not get better.

I challenge each and every one of you today to make the best out of every situation that you will face. Grab fear by the horns and toss them aside as if it were nothing. I believe in you and all that you can achieve.

Chapter 26:

Why You're Demotivated By Lack of Clarity

Clarity is key to achieving any lasting happiness or success.

Demotivation is almost certain without clarity.

Always have a clear vision of what you want and why you want it.

Every detail should be crystal clear as if it were real.

Because it is.

Mustn't reality first be built on a solid foundation of imagination.

Your skills in visualisation and imagination must be strong to build that foundation.

You must build it in the mind and focus on it daily.

You must believe in it with all your heart and your head will follow.

Create it in the mind and let your body build it in reality.

That is the process of creation.

You cannot create anything in reality without clarity in the mind.

Even to make a cup of coffee, you must first imagine making a cup of coffee.

It doesn't take as much clarity as creating an international company,

but focus and clarity are required nonetheless.

The big goals often take years of consistent focus, clarity and commitment.

That is why so few succeed.

Demotivation is a symptom of lack of direction.

To have direction you must have clarity.

To have clarity you must have a clearly defined vision of you future.

Once you have this vision, never accept anything less.

Clarity and vision will begin your journey,

but your arrival depends on stubbornness and persistence.

Before you start you must decide to never quit, no matter what happens.

Clarity of your why will decide this for you.

Is the pain you are about to endure stronger than your reasons?

If you are currently demoralised by lack of clarity,

sit down and decide what will really make you happy.

Once you have decided, begin to make it feel real with pictures around your house.

Listen to motivational music and speeches daily to build your belief in you.

Visit where you dream you will be one day.

Get a feel for your desired new life.

Create actions that will build clarity in your vision.

Let it help you adjust to your new and future reality.

Slowly adjust your vision upwards.

Never adjust downwards.

Never settle for less.

The more real your vision feels the more likely it will be.

Begin to visualise living it.

Before long you will be living it.

Adopt the mannerisms of someone who would be in that position.

When you begin to believe you are important, others will follow.

Carry yourself like a champion.

Soon you will be one.

Have clarity you have about who you are.

Have clarity about what you are going to do.

Motivate yourself to success.

Once you step on that path you will not want to return to the you of yesterday.

You will be committed to becoming even better tomorrow.

You will be committed to being the new person you've always known you could be.

Always strive to get another step closer to your vision.

Work until that vision becomes clearer each day.

Have faith that each week more opportunities for progression will present themselves to you.

Clarity is the key to your success.

Chapter 27:

Share Your Troubles Freely and Openly

Life is hard. We go through tons of challenges, problems, and obstacles every single day. We accumulate problems and stresses left right and Center. Absorbing each impact blow for blow.

Over time, these impacts will wear us down mentally and physically. Without a proper release channel, we find that our emotions spill over in ways when we least expect it. We get easily irritated, have a hard time falling asleep, have mood issues, and find ourselves even being temporarily depressed at times.

When we bottle negativity, it festers inside us without us realising what we have done. That is where releasing those tensions by pouring our heart and soul into friends, writing, journaling, and other outlets that allow us to express our feelings freely without judgement.

We may not all have friends that we can truly count on to share our deepest darkest secrets for fear that they might share these secrets unsuspectingly. If we do have these types of friends, treasure them and seek them out regularly to share your problems. By bouncing ideas off someone, we may even find a new solution to an old problem that we couldn't before. The other party may also be able to see things more objectively and with a unique perspective that is contrary to yours which you could potentially use to your advantage.

If writing things down is something that helps you cope with life, then by all means take a piece of paper and write down all the things that have been bothering you. Journal it, archive it. You may even write a song about it if that helps you process things better. Writing things down help us clear our minds and lets us see the big picture when we come back to it at a later date should we feel ready to address it. When things are too crazy, we may not have the mental capacity to handle everything being thrown at us at one go. So take the time to sort those feelings out.

You may also choose to just find a place that brings you relaxation. Whether it be going to the beach, or renting a hotel, or even just screaming at the top of your lungs. Let those feelings out. Don't keep it hidden inside.

IF all these things still don't work for you, you may want to try seeking help from a professional counsellor or therapist who can work out these issues you have in your life one by one. Never be afraid to book an appointment because your mental health is more important than the stigma associated with seeing a professional. You are not admitting you have a problem, you are simply acknowledge that there are areas in your life that you need assistance with. And that it is perfectly okay and perfectly normal to do so. Counsellors have the passion to serve, the passion to help, and that is why they chose that profession to being with. So seek their assistance and guidance as much as you need to.

Life isn't easy. But we can all take a conscious effort to regulate our emotions more healthily to live a long and balanced life.

Chapter 28:

How To Start Working Immediately

"There is only one way for me to motivate myself to work hard: I don't think about it as hard work. I think about it as part of making myself into who I want to be. Once I've chosen to do something, I try not to think so much about how difficult or frustrating or impossible that might be; I just think about how good it must feel to be that or how proud I might be to have done that. Make hard look easy." - Marie Stein.

Motivation is somewhat elusive. Some days you feel it naturally, other days you don't, no matter how hard you try. You stare at your laptop screen or your essay at the desk, willing yourself to type or write; instead, you find yourself simply going through the motions, not caring about the work that you're producing. You're totally uninspired, and you don't know how to make yourself feel otherwise. You find yourself being dissatisfied, discouraged, frustrated, or disappointed to get your hands on those long-awaited tasks. While hoping for things to change and make our lives better overnight magically, we waste so much of our precious time. Sorry to burst your bubble, but things just don't happen like that. You have to push yourself off that couch, turn off the phone, switch off Netflix and make it happen. There's no need to seek anyone's permission or blessings to start your work.

The world doesn't care about how tired you are. Or, if you're feeling depressed or anxious, stop feeling sorry for yourself while you're at it. It doesn't matter one bit. We all face obstacles and challenges and struggles throughout our days, but how we deal with those obstacles and difficulties defines us and our successes in life. As James Clear once said, "Professionals stick to the schedule, amateurs let life get in the way. Professionals know what is important to them and work towards it with purpose; amateurs get pulled off course by the urgencies of life."

Take a deep breath. Brew in your favorite coffee. Eat something healthy. Take a shower, take a walk, talk to someone who lifts your energy, turn off your socials, and when you're done with all of them, set your mind straight and start working immediately. Think about the knowledge, the skill, the experience that you'll gain from working. Procrastination might feel good but imagine how amazing it will feel when you'll finally get your tasks, your work done. Don't leave anything for tomorrow. Start doing it today. We don't know what tomorrow might bring for us. If we will be able even to wake up and breathe. We don't know it for sure. So, start hustling today. You just need that activation energy to start your chain of events.

Start scheduling your work on your calendar and actually follow it. We may feel like we have plenty of time to get things done. Hence, we tend to ignore our work and take it easy. But to tell you the truth, time flickers by in seconds. Before you know it, you're already a week behind your deadline, and you still haven't started working yet. Keep reminding yourself as to why you need to do this work done. Define your goals and get them into action. Create a clear and compelling vision of your work. You only achieve what you see. Break your work into small, manageable tasks so you stay motivated throughout your work procedure. Get yourself organized. Unclutter your mind. Starve your distractions. Create that perfect environment so you can keep up with your work until you're done. Please choose to be successful and then stick to it.

You may feel like you're fatigued, or your mind will stop producing ideas and creativity after a while. But that's completely fine. Take a break. Set a timer for five minutes. Force yourself to work on the thing for five minutes, and after those five minutes, it won't feel too bad to keep going. Make a habit of doing the small tasks first, so they get out of the way, and you can harness your energy to tackle the more significant projects.

Reward yourself every time you complete your work. This will boost your confidence and will give you the strength to continue with your remaining tasks. Don't let your personal and professional responsibilities overwhelm you. Help yourself stay focused by keeping in mind that you're accountable for your own actions. Brian Roemmele, the Quora user, encourages people to own every moment, "You are in full control of this power. In your hands, you can build the tallest building and, in your hands, you can destroy the tallest buildings."

Start surrounding yourself with people who are an optimist and works hard. The saying goes, you're the average of the five people you hang out with the most. So, make sure you surround yourself with people who push you to succeed.

No matter how uninspired or de-motivating it may seem, you have to take that first step and start working. Whether it's a skill that you're learning, a language that you want to know, a dance step that you wish to perfect, a business idea that you want to implement, an instrument that you want to master, or simply doing the work for anyone else, you should do it immediately. Don't wait for the next minute, the next hour, the next day, or the following week; start doing your stuff. No one else is going to do your work for you, nor it's going to be completed by itself. Only you have the power to get on with it and get it done. Get your weak spots fixed. In the end, celebrate your achievements whether it's small or big. Imagine the relief of not having that task up on your plate anymore. Visualize yourself succeeding. It can help you stay to stay focused and motivated and get your work done. Even the worst tasks won't feel painful, but instead, they'll feel like a part of achieving something big.

Remember, motivation starts within. Find it, keep it and make it work wonders for you.

Chapter 29:

Hitting Rock Bottom

Today we're going to talk about a topic that I hope none of you will have to experience at any point in your lives. It can be a devastating and painful experience and I don't wish it on my worst enemy, but if this happens to be you, I hope that in today's video I can help you get out of the depths and into the light again.

First of all, I'm not going to waste any more time but just tell you that hitting rock bottom could be your blessing in disguise. You see when we hit rock bottom, the only reason that we know we are there is because we have become aware and have admitted to ourselves that there is no way lower that we can go. That we know deep in our hearts that things just cannot get any worse than this. And that revelation can be enlightening. Enlightening in the sense that by simple law of physics, the worse that can happen moving forward is either you move sideways, or up. When you have nothing more left to lose, you can be free to try and do everything in your power to get back up again.

For a lot of us who have led pretty comfortable lives, sometimes it feels like we are living in a bubble. We end up drifting through life on the comforts of our merits that we fail to stop learning and growing as people. We become so jaded about everything that life becomes bland.

We stop trying to be better, we stop trying to care, and we that in itself could be poison. It is like a frog getting boiled gradually, we don't notice it until it is too late and we are cooked. We are in fact slowly dying and fading into irrelevance.

But when you are at rock bottom, you become painfully aware of everything. Painfully aware of maybe your failed relationships, the things you did and maybe the people you hurt that have led you to this point. You become aware that you need to change yourself first, that everything starts with growing and learning again from scratch, like a baby learning how to walk again. And that could be a very rewarding time in your life when you become virtually fearless to try and do anything in your power to get back on your feet again.

Of course all this has to come from you. That you have to make the decision that things will never stay the same again. That you will learn from your mistakes and do the right things. When you've hit rock bottom, you can slowly begin the climb one step at a time.

Start by defining the first and most important thing that you cannot live without in life. If family means the most to you, reach out to them. Find comfort and shelter in them and see if they are able to provide you with any sort of assistance while you work on your life again. I always believe that if family is the most important thing, and that people you call family will be there with you till the very end. If family is not available to you, make it a priority to start growing a family. Family doesn't mean you have to have blood relations. Family is whoever you can rely on in your darkest times. Family is people who will accept you and love you for who you are inspite of your shortcomings. Family is people that will help nurture and get you back on your own two feet again. If you don't have family, go get one.

If hitting rock bottom to you means that you feel lost in life, in your career and finance, that you maybe lost your businesses and are dealing with the aftermath, maybe your first priority is to simply find a simple part time job that can occupy your time and keep you sustained while you figure out what to do next. Sometimes all we need is a little break to clear our heads and to start afresh again. Nothing ever stays the same. Things will get better. But don't fall into the trap of ruminating on your losses as it can be very destructive on your mental health. The past has already happened and you cannot take it back. Take stock of the reasons and don't make the same mistakes again in your career and you will be absolutely fine.

If you feel like you've hit rock bottom because of a failed marriage or relationship, whether it be something you did or your partner did, I know this can be incredibly painful and it feels like you've spent all your time with someone with nothing to show for it but wasted time and energy, but know that things like that happen and that it is perfectly normal. Humans are flawed and we all make mistakes. So yes it is okay to morn over the loss of the relationship and feel like you can't sink any lower, but don't lose faith as you will find someone again.

If hitting rock bottom is the result of you being ostracised by people around you for not being a good person, where you maybe have lost all the relationships in your life because of something you did, I'm sure you know the first step to do is to accept that you need to change. Don't look to someone else to blame but look inwards instead. Find time where you can go away on your way to reflect on what went wrong. Start going through the things that people were unhappy with you about and start looking for ways to improve yourself. If you need help, I am here for you. If not, maybe you might want to seek some professional help as well to dig a little deeper and to help guide you along a better path.

Hitting rock bottom is not a fun thing, and I don't want to claim that I know every nuance and feeling of what it means to get there, but I did feel like that once when my business failed on me and I made the decision that I could only go up from here. I started to pour all my time and energy into proving to myself that I will succeed no matter what and that I will not sit idly by and feel sorry for myself. It was a quite a journey but I came out of it stronger than before and realized that I was more resourceful than I originally thought.

So I challenge each and everyone of you who feels like you've hit the bottom to not be afraid of taking action once again. To be fearless and just take that next right step forward no matter what. And I hope to see you on the top of the mountain in time to come.

Chapter 30:

Overcoming Fear and Self-Doubt

The lack of belief most people have is the reason for their failure at even the smallest things in life. The biggest killer of dreams is the lack of belief in ourselves and the doubt of failure.

We all make mistakes. We all have some ghosts of the past that haunt us. We all have something to hide. We all have something that we regret. But what you are today is not the result of your mistakes.

You are here because of your struggles to make those things go away. You are here now with the power and strength to shape your present and your future.

Our mind is designed to take the shape of what we hold long enough inside it. The things we frequently think about ultimately start filling in the spaces within our memory, so we have to be careful. We have to decide whether we want to stay happy or to hold on to the fear we once wanted to get rid of.

The human spirit and human soul are colored by the impressions we ourselves decide to impose.

The reason why we don't want to explore the possibility of what to do is that subconsciously we don't believe that it can happen for us. We don't believe that we deserve it or if it was meant for us.

So here is something I suggest. Ask yourself, how much time in a day do you spend thinking about your dream? How much time do you spend working on your dreams everyday? What books did you read this year? What new skills have you acquired recently? What have you done that makes you worthy of your dream? Nothing?

Then you are on point with your doubt because you don't have anything to show for when the opportunity presents itself.

You don't succeed because you have this latent fear. Fear that makes you think about the consequences of what will happen if you fail even with all the good things on your hand?

I know that feeling but failure is there to teach you one important and maybe the most essential skill life can teach us; Resilience.

You rediscover your life once you have the strength to fight your every fear and every doubt because you have better things on your hand to care for.

You have another dream to pursue. Another horizon awaits you. Another peak to summit. It doesn't matter if you literally have to run to stand still. You got to do what you got to do, no matter the consequences and the sacrifices.

But failing to do what is required of you has no justifiable defense. Not even fear. Because your fears are self-imposed and you already have many wrong things going on for you right now.

Don't let fear be one of them. Because fear is the most subtle and destructive disease So inhale all your positive energies and exhale all your doubts because you certainly are a better person without them.

Chapter 31:

Achieving Happiness

Happiness is a topic that is at the core of this channel. Because as humans we all want to be happy in some way shape or form. Happiness strikes as something that we all want to strive for because how can we imagine living an unhappy life. It might be possible but it wouldn't be all that fun no matter how you spin it. However I'm gonna offer another perspective that would challenge the notion of happiness and one that maybe would be more attainable for the vast majority of people.

So why do we as humans search for happiness? It is partly due to the fact that it has been ingrained in us since young that we all should strive to live a happy and healthy life. Happiness has become synonymous with the very nature of existence that when we find ourselves unhappy in any given moment, we tend to want to pivot our life and the current situation we are in to one that is more favourable, one that is supposedly able to bring us more happiness.

But how many of us are actually always happy all the time? I would argue that happiness is not at all sustainable if we were feeling it at full blast constantly. After a while we would find ourselves being numb to it and maybe that happiness would turn into neutrality or even boredom. There were times in my life where i felt truly happy and free. I felt that i had great friends around me, life had limitless possibilities, the weather was great, the housing situation was great, and i never wanted it to end as i knew that it was the best time of my life.

However knowing that this circumstance is only temporary allowed me to cherish each and every moment more meaningfully. As i was aware that time was not infinite and that some day this very state of happiness would somehow end one way or another, that i would use that time wisely and spend them with purpose and meaning. And it was this sense that nothing ever lasts forever that helped me gain a new perspective on everything i was doing at that present moment in time. Of course, those happy times were also filled with times of trials, conflicts, and challenges, and they made that period of my life all the more memorable and noteworthy.

For me, happiness is a temporary state that does not last forever. We might be happy today but sad tomorrow, but that is perfectly okay and totally fine. Being happy all the time is not realistic no matter how you spin it. The excitement of getting a new house and new car would soon fade from the moment you start driving in it, and that happiness you once thought you associated with it can disappear very quickly. And that is okay. Because life is about constant change and nothing really ever stays the same.

With happiness comes with it a whole host of different emotions that aims to highlight and enhance its feeling. Without sadness and sorrow, happiness would have no counter to be matched against. It is like a yin without a yang. And we need both in order to survive.

I believe that to be truly happy, one has to accept that sadness and feelings of unhappiness will come as a package deal. That whilst we want to be happy, we must also want to feel periods of lull to make the experience more rewarding.

I challenge all of you today to view happiness as not something that is static and that once you achieved it that all will be well and life will be good, but rather a temporary state of feeling that will come again and again when you take steps to seek it.

Chapter 32:

Overcome Demotivation

Human life is very short and keeps getting shorter and shorter with each day. In this short life we feel discouraged and every other moment or every other day. We get frustrated and we tend to lose hope.

But then good days come too and we feel on top of the world. Our hearts are overfilled with joy and satisfaction but this too lasts for some time and then life surprises us with some new big rock of grief or depression. This moment though short can take us down a deep hole where we don't see a way back up.

This is the moment of everyone's life where they are the most demotivated to do anything in life. No matter how much our loved ones try to get us to try one more time, we keep sinking deeper into self-rejection and denial.

This feeling of not being motivated no matter what good comes around time after time is not helpful for anyone even if you need to become the world's most successful person.

But there are countless things you can do to deviate your mind from any such situation. Let's discuss some.

I'll say, you get up right away, tighten up some shoes and get out on a long run. Try to look around you and find anyone else who can apparently be in any distress. Approach them if you can and help them in any way possible if they allow you to.

Try to feel others' pain and surely you will be thankful for what you already have in life.

If you don't feel like going out that's OK too; pick up the phone and call anyone who you think might care for the most for what you are going through right now. If you have someone who can relate to you in such times of greys and blacks, you surely have an escape route.

You might think you are sitting alone on your couch in your sweats and wandering over random things to take your mind off.

But the reality is that every now and then in such alone moments you wander off in conditions where you somehow end up comparing yourself with someone else and rather than being inspired by that person, you feel jealous and might curse someone. You start to think what they have is perfect and you can never be there. But the reality is they are there because they knew how to overcome these feelings you have right now.

So reorder yourself. Make a new plan. Make a new scheme for what you should be doing when the next fire breaks in your life. What you can do to overcome the next rejection.

Things have always a way to release you. Events can leave an impact but that impact doesn't necessarily have to stamp rather a lesson to take new paths. You don't want to put your hands in the same hole again where you were once bitten. You just need to find a way to get around the hole and keep the track you were once on!

Chapter 33:

Live A Long, Important Life

Do you think you are more capable to deal with the failure or the regret of not trying at all?

Are you living the life you want or the life everyone else wants for you?

Would you feel good spending your time on entertainment that might not last for long? Or would you feel good feeling like you are growing and have a better self of you to look at in the mirror?

Similarly, would like to live in the present or would you love to work for a better future?

Do you want money to dictate your life or do you want money to follow you where ever you go?

Would you prefer being tired or being broke?

Do you want to spend the rest of your life in this place where you and your parents were born? Or do you won't go around the world and find new possibilities in even the most remote places?

Would you rather risk it all or play it safe?

We are often presented with all these questions in our lifetime. Most people take these questions as a way to enter into your adulthood. The answers to these questions are meant to show you the actual meaning of life.

So what is Life? Life is not your parents, your work, your friends, your events, and your functions. It's within you and around you.

You should learn to live your life to the fullest. You should love to live your life for as long as you can with a happy body and a healthy mind.

A happy and healthy body and mind are important. Because you can only feel secure on a stable platform. You can only wish to stand on a platform where you know you can stay put for a long time.

There is nothing wrong with working eight or nine hours in your daily life. It's not unhealthy or anything. Working is what gives our life a purpose. Working is what keeps us active, moving, and motivated.

We have one life, and we have to make it matter. But the way we chose to do it is what matters the most. Our choices make us who we are rather than our actions.

The life we live is the epitome of our intentions and morals. We can be defined in a single word or a single phrase if we ever try. We don't need to analyze someone else, we just need to see ourselves in the mirror and we might be able to see right across the image.

The day we are able to do that, might be the day we have actually made a worthy human being of ourselves and have fulfilled our destiny.

If you are able to look at yourself and go through your whole life in the blink of an eye and cherish the memories as if you were right there at that moment. Believe me, you have had a long and important life to make you think of it all over again every day.

CPSIA information can be obtained
at www.ICGtesting.com
Printed in the USA
LVHW050741260122
709198LV00008B/331